To Sister Mary Lamski, CSJ,
my second grade teacher —B.P.C.

To Lisa, Cam and Rosie —J.P.

Millbrook Press
A division of Lerner Publishing Group, Inc.
241 First Avenue North
Minneapolis, MN 55401 USA

For reading levels and more information, look up this title at www.lernerbooks.com.

Main body text set in Bawdy Regular 18/26.
Typeface provided by Chank.

Library of Congress Cataloging-in-Publication Data

Cleary, Brian P., 1959– author.
    They're there on their vacation / Brian P. Cleary ; Illustrations by Jim Paillot.
        pages cm. — (Millbrook Picture Books)
    Audience: K to Grade 3.
    ISBN 978-0-7613-9033-6 (lb : alk. paper) — ISBN 978-1-4677-8847-2 (eb pdf)
    1. English language—Homonyms—Juvenile literature. I. Paillot, Jim, illustrator.
PE1595.C585 2015
    428.1—dc23   2014041284

Manufactured in the United States of America
1 – DP – 7/15/15

They're There on Their Vacation

Brian P. Cleary

Illustrations by Jim Paillot

Millbrook Press / Minneapolis

In town, **there** lives a family.
Their name is Tuckabee.
They're not the type who like resorts,
the mountains, or the sea.

And so when they vacation,
their mission is to find
a place that's quite unusual,
then go **there** to unwind.

The kids? **They're** in the car.
They ask **their** parents, "Are we **there**?"
while on **their** way to see
the World's Largest Underwear.

"**They're** absolutely giant,"
says **their** youngest, Mary Claire.
"In all the land, **there** couldn't be
a more enormous pair."

"**There**'s sixty pounds of cotton and elastic, and **they're** sewn with sixteen thousand stitches," says **their** docent, Ms. Malone.

Next, **they're** on the road to see the Narwhal Petting Zoo.

Their Grandma Tuckabee is **there**
to meet up with the crew.

"**There** aren't too many folks in line,"
their grandma says to Mark.
"**They're** all across the street at
that enormous water park."

SPLASH MANIA

enter

Mom and Dad take photographs
of Grandma and **their** kids,
who feed the long-tusked mammals
bits of fishes, shrimps, and squids.

Next stop, for an overnight,
they're happy to arrive
at Indoor Acres Camping Ground
right **there** off 95.

"It's air-conditioned," says **their** mom.
"No sunburn, no mosquitoes—
with stores **there** that sell everything
from bear claws to burritos."

With microwaves to make **their** s'mores
or heat **their** franks and beans,
they're camping in the great indoors—
complete with ice machines!

"**There's** time for spooky stories now,"
says Mark to Mary Claire.
While watching his TV, Dad says,
"Kids, get some sleep in **there**."

The last stop on **their** list this year? **They're** driving north to see how Cheezie Popz are made inside **their** awesome factory.

They're singing and they're playing games
until Mark stops to say,
"Look! You guys—we'll be **there** soon!
It's just five miles away!"

There are three huge tanks **they're** filling
with corn and oil and cheeses
that splert out on conveyor belts
in puffs like tiny sneezes.

Inside **their** space-age Puffing Room,
the blobs are shot with air.
So now **they're** light and floaty
as they bob about in **there**.

They're powdered in **their** special room.
They're counted, bagged, and weighed.
"And that," declares **their** expert,
"is how Cheezie Popz are made."

With **their** vacation now complete, **they're** all discussing where they'll take **their** next vacation, and they can't wait to go **there**!

More about They're, There, and Their

Even in the title of this book, **there** are three words that sound a lot alike. **They're** homophones—words that are spelled differently but pronounced the same. **Their** meanings are different, though, and **they're** used for different purposes.

They're is a contraction, or shortened version, of the words *they are*. So if the phrase "they are" makes sense in the sentence you're writing, you can use "**they're**" instead.
Example: **They're** going to Mars.

There describes a place. Sometimes the place is a physical location. Sometimes it's an abstract, or imaginary, place. You can also use this word just to say that something exists.
Examples:
Put the monkey **there**.
He should've stopped right **there**, but he just kept talking.
There is a lot of work to do.

Their shows ownership. It describes things that "they" have.
Example: The kids took out **their** books.

Now that you've read this book, I hope **there** will be no more confusion!